Despair to Joy

A Bipolar Woman's Quest For Wholeness

Ann Perkins With Wanda Goerz

Copyright © 2010 Wanda Goerz

All rights reserved. No part of this book may be used or reproduced by any means, graphic, electronic, or mechanical, including photocopying, recording, taping or by any information storage retrieval system without the written permission of the publisher except in the case of brief quotations embodied in critical articles and reviews.

WestBow Press books may be ordered through booksellers or by contacting:

WestBow Press
A Division of Thomas Nelson
1663 Liberty Drive
Bloomington, IN 47403
www.westbowpress.com
1-(866) 928-1240

Because of the dynamic nature of the Internet, any Web addresses or links contained in this book may have changed since publication and may no longer be valid. The views expressed in this work are solely those of the author and do not necessarily reflect the views of the publisher, and the publisher hereby disclaims any responsibility for them.

Any people depicted in stock imagery provided by Thinkstock are models, and such images are being used for illustrative purposes only.

Certain stock imagery © Thinkstock.

ISBN: 978-1-4497-0972-3 (sc)
ISBN: 978-1-4497-0973-0 (e)

Library of Congress Control Number: 2010941433

Printed in the United States of America

WestBow Press rev. date: 12/29/2010

To my precious daughters:
Karol Ann
&
Debbie

Contents

Preface	ix
Introduction	xi
Pampered and Loved	1
Setting Out With My Life Mate	7
The Honeymoon Ended	11
A Cry For Help	15
My First Hospitalization	17
In Sickness and in Health	20
Sustaining Faith	26
A Breakthrough At Last	34
The Great Unraveling	38
Spiritual Formation	44
Successful Transition	47
My Own Business	50
More Health Problems	52
Karol's Last Days	54
Epilogue	59
Suggested Resources	61
Notes	63

Preface

When Ann first saw me, she had already seen two or three psychiatrists and had taken six or eight psychiatric medications. She was frightened, angry and desperate. She had decided that if taking pills to get what, if any, relief they may give was all that she had to look forward to, she didn't want to go on living. She recently had made one or two threats and superficial attempts at suicide.

Not only was Ann frightened, angry and desperate, she was also excitable, flighty and didn't like herself. She no longer knew which way to turn, or what to do. She had sought the help of her pastor, but she had caused two or three "scenes" at the church and her pastor no longer knew what to do to help her. He recommended that she see a doctor and get some medication. Thus started our regular long and formal period of treatment/therapy, a relationship that we've been privileged to continue in a less frequent and intense manner.

Ann's low self-esteem resulted from mistaken teaching and example at home and at church, and of having years of undiagnosed and untreated severe mental illness. At home she had been over protected and over directed; at church she had been taught that "good Christians" never draw attention to themselves, nor do they brag on themselves. She was also taught to model joy and to put Jesus first; others second; and self last.

Ann was a committed believer, an active church member and an eager, earnest patient. She took a six or eight month "breather" from her church, and started a daily regimen of intensive prayer, medication, reading, studying and journaling. We began to meet together an hour or so each week. Gradually Ann began to slowly stabilize, grow and improve personally, emotionally, spiritually and in her relationships. Her physical health improved more slowly.

She credits her healing and recovery to having found a "Christian Psychiatrist." I wholeheartedly agree that therapy which valued and respected the healthy aspects of her spirituality, while helping her identify the unhealthy aspects was as significant to her recovery as were the psychiatric medications that she took and still takes.

Twenty or thirty years ago, when Ann began her therapy, psychiatry had begun to replace talking and relationship building with psychiatric medications to treat "chemical imbalances." But to this day, there are still no "chemical imbalances" that can be detected in the central nervous system.

In the last ten to fifteen years, a rebalancing of talking and relating with psychiatric medication has occurred. Psychiatric medication and various cognitive therapies have proven to give the best results. Wrong thoughts can and must be changed if emotional healing is to take place. ". . . As a man thinks in his heart, so is he."[1] Over time, Ann changed her thinking. Her willingness to learn to think differently made the desired balance possible. It is my hope and prayer that Ann's story will add to this rebalancing.

John H. Freer, MD

Introduction

By writing my story, I am fulfilling a strong need to tell others with bipolar disorder that they can progress beyond temporary, leveled-out moods. More than that, they can live joyful, peaceful, productive lives, with recovered functioning in more of the wholeness that God intends for us all.

I was diagnosed with bipolar disorder, also known as manic depressive disorder, when I was twenty-nine years old. It held me in its grip for fifteen years before I received treatment beyond medication. On average, it takes seven years for bipolar illness to be diagnosed. The delay is thought to result from the tendency of patients to report only their depressive symptoms while failing to mention their manic episodes. By the time I found a psychiatrist who also offered Christian psychiatric counseling, I had become emotionally crippled as well as mentally dysfunctional. My relationships were disturbed, as were life events within the nature and nurture of my experience.

Bipolar disorder is believed to be triggered by an imbalance of some key chemicals in the brain. Cells release chemicals known as neurotransmitters which are essential to brain function. When the levels of these neurotransmitters are too high or too low, bipolar disorder may manifest itself in any of the following ways: Excessive talking; making unwise, grandiose plans; taking foolish risks; exhibiting extreme happiness, irritability, sadness, lack of energy and frequent depression. Without diagnosis and treatment, the symptoms worsen as a person ages.

Once my dramatic mood swings were curbed with medication, my damaged emotions had to be dealt with. No doubt, many other bipolar sufferers have serious emotional difficulties as well, particularly if they are diagnosed long after their first symptoms occur. Throughout history, we've heard of many famous people having frequent and dramatic mood swings. Perhaps the best documented example is Sir Winston Churchill who called his episodes of deep depression his "Black Dog." Others are Mary Todd Lincoln, Beethoven, Vincent Van Gogh and Sir Isaac Newton.

Performers Connie Frances, Patty Duke, and Carrie Fisher have joined the ranks of celebrities who have revealed their struggles as bipolar sufferers. The condition is no respecter of status, gender, or ethnic origin. More accurate diagnoses are possible today, and it has been learned that there are several classifications of bipolar disorder. The stigma of mental illness is gradually beginning to lift; therefore it is more openly discussed. This has probably made us tend to think that the disorder has suddenly grown much more common. However, statistics do indicate that diagnosed cases are on the rise.

Within the past five years, increasing numbers of individuals from ordinary walks of life have written their stories about living with the challenging condition. Most seldom mention spirituality as having any role in their recovery. The current definition of recovery as it applies to bipolar disorder is attaining a peaceful mental state, free of mood swings. That does not mean free of medical treatment. Medical science and psychotherapy are usually given total credit when a bipolar individual recovers. By fully placing my faith in Christ, I was able to discern a definite direction to seek the professional services of a Christian psychiatrist. Only then did I finally come through the thick maze of manic depressive confusion and dysfunction to a place where I recognized the power, mercy and grace of our loving God who stood ready to nurture me beyond mere contentment to a place of peace and joy. Despite several seasons of adversity, I have remained in this state through two decades.

Any one of the later crisis situations would have brought me down had they occurred before I received adequate medical treatment, psychotherapy and spiritual direction. Don't misunderstand me. Medicine and psychotherapy are essential treatments, and usually a bipolar individual needs both before being able to focus on anyone but them self. It will become apparent as you read my story that I place a heavy emphasis on the fact that faith in God was the sustaining force that led to my recovery. The peace, joy and love within my heart can never be taken away. I now know that I must always continue on medication that is regularly monitored.

The focus of my writing is not on the scientific cause and treatment of bipolar disorder. That must be left to professionals. However, I do focus on family dynamics, social interaction, coping mechanisms of my family and my own, and most importantly, the role of a strong faith. I must credit my psychiatrist, Dr. John H. Freer, MD for insisting on spiritual formation as an essential part of my growing into the plan that God had for my life before I was conceived in my mother's womb.

Whether or not one is bipolar, spiritual growth is a lifelong endeavor. Sufferers of the disorder must find a professional who will first: guide them into an individually tailored medical regimen to control extreme mood swings. The mood swings, of course, are the most prevalent characteristic of the disorder. Then, it is usually necessary that the patient receives psychotherapy for emotional dysfunction. This, more often than not, requires the patient to change long-held wrong thinking. It is a slow process. Unless the two steps of treatment are provided in sequence, then later simultaneously, disciplines necessary for spiritual growth are blocked. I sought help long before I found the right individual. I encourage anyone who has been unsuccessful in finding that right doctor to persevere in their search. It is my prayer that through my story, others will be encouraged in their quest for recovery.

Pampered and Loved

My mother, Hallie Brock, was born in 1899, the eldest of ten children. She grew up on a Kentucky farm just outside of Lexington in the community of Avon. Her parents saw to it that she and her six sisters and three brothers attended church as faithfully as they milked the cows and performed other farm chores. At fourteen, Hallie accepted Christ and began a life of dedicated service, prayer and tithing.

Hallie graduated from Berea High School. She had no intention of furthering her education because she had convinced herself that she lacked the intelligence to succeed beyond high school level. In those days, particularly in the area where she grew up, young women were not encouraged to attend college. Hallie was working in Berea when she met Edward Cox, a young pharmacy student. He convinced her that indeed, she was capable of obtaining an education to prepare her for the nursing career that she had only dreamed about.

With Edward's encouragement and support, Hallie paid her way through nursing school by earning six or seven dollars per month. She began her training at Good Samaritan Hospital in Lexington, and finished at Deaconess Hospital in Louisville. Meanwhile, Hallie and Edward had fallen deeply in love. Marriage plans had to be put on hold though, since student nurses were not allowed to marry during the time they were in training. Then, Hallie's handsome fiancé was stricken with pneumonia. Unfortunately, he refused to stop working and died almost on his feet. The grieving young woman, just twenty-three-years-old, relied on her strong faith to carry her through. She finished her training, as did her sister Verna who had been with Ed at his death. By this time her family had moved to Hazard. Hallie moved there also, and took a job at the local hospital.

Hazard, founded in 1790 was named after U. S. Navy Commodore Oliver Hazard Perry. Perry was known for his victory report during the War of 1812, when he stated, "We have met the enemy and they are ours." Many think of the CBS television series, *The Dukes of Hazzard* when they hear of Hazard, Kentucky. Indeed, the show which ran from 1979-1985 did get its name from the eastern Kentucky town, but to avoid legal problems, producers of the popular comedy added an extra "z," and set the show in a fictional county in Georgia.[2]

Historically, there have been many generous, imaginative, and creative residents of Hazard and Perry County. One such person was George Stacy, a railroad worker. Stacy amazed his wife, Ollie, when he came up with an idea to build a goose-shaped house. The story goes that Stacy had no training and no house plan. Before he could begin building his dream project, he went goose hunting and killed a large goose. Then, he asked his wife to cook it and take off all of the meat. She was to leave the skeleton intact. Stacy then used the goose skeleton as a scale. The roof of the Mother Goose house has ribs just like a goose. The body of the building resembles a nest and the windows are egg shaped. Auto headlamps serve as the goose's eyes. The Mother Goose house took five years to complete and it served as home for the Stacy family for many years. It still stands just as it was a half century ago when Stacy died. Tourist still can't resist pulling over to the side of the road and taking a picture of the unusual building. However, natives of the area never think of it as being unusual. It is more a normal part of the landscape.

Lawrence Davis and his wife built several landmarks in the Hazard community to memorialize their son Bobby who was killed at the end of WWII. La Citadel, a hotel and restaurant was probably the most famous. Every room provided a panoramic view of the beautiful mountain environs. The road leading to the place was so steep that it felt like a roller coaster incline. La Citadel's motto was: "Looking down on the stars." Indeed, Hazard can boast of several interesting and unique structures. Hallie soon adapted to her new community, and came to feel at home in Hazard. While few travelers came through the small town, she met many people through her work at the hospital. One of her patients was a six-year-old girl suffering with a serious bout of influenza. The child's uncle, Harve Engle, came to visit his niece. While there, he met the caring, petite nurse, Hallie.

He saw in her a reason to go on living. Harve was an embalmer who, only two months earlier, lost his wife and their first baby in childbirth.

Both, having experienced loss of first loves, thought it best not to rush into marriage. Harve also suffered from tuberculosis and feared the disease would adversely affect his ability to provide for his family. Some of his fear, no doubt, was rooted in the rawness of loosing his first family. Nevertheless, when both were thirty-years-old, they married and began housekeeping in the Mattie Belle Apartment House in Hazard.

The Great Depression continued into 1935, and unemployment was 20.1%. As if there was not already enough bleakness, war clouds were gathering in Germany. Yet the country was united when it came to sympathy for world famous aviator Charles Lindberg and his wife, whose twenty-two-month-old baby boy had been kidnapped and murdered. Bruno Hauptmann had recently been convicted and charged with the crime. In the same year, Harve and Hallie brought me into the world. It is possible that my parents were more protective of me than they may have been had they not known that the Lindberg baby was stolen from his second floor crib early one evening, and brutally murdered.

For whatever reason, I was an only child, although I envied others who had siblings to play with. My mother claimed that she was too old to have another baby. Another likely factor in their decision was that Daddy's tuberculosis worsened. I was less than two-years-old when our family moved to Louisville so that Daddy could enter Waverly Hills Sanatorium where he stayed for an entire year. Upon his release, we returned to Hazard, settling in the Flatwoods community. The area was so isolated that only one house was in walking distance. Daddy doted on me and I adored him. I was especially thrilled when he built a big sandbox for me. When my young cousin needed eye glasses, I was green with envy. I said, "Daddy, I can't see the side of a barn." He placated me by punching out the lenses of some old sunglasses and letting me wear just the frames.

Sometimes Daddy allowed me to accompany him to the post office. I felt special just being with Daddy, but getting to see the postmaster's son who was about my age, was an additional pleasure. Once heavy rains washed out the bridge and we had to retrieve our mail by boat. No child ever felt more adventuresome than I when Daddy allowed me to accompany him and help paddle the boat through the murky waters to the post office.

Unfortunately, Daddy's tuberculosis worsened. I was five-years-old when he and Mother decided to move to Texas where the climate was said to speed the cure of tuberculosis. They owned a life insurance policy with a medical rider which adequately supported us during that time. Texas was an unpleasant experience for me. Because the children in the community were unknown to my parents, they kept me inside most of the time. However, the Texas climate did heal Daddy's lungs, and a year later we were able to return to Hazard.

During Daddy's absence, his brother with whom he partnered in a funeral home and floral business brought his son into the business and my father was ousted. He probably believed that Daddy would never be able to contribute his share to the operation. Nevertheless, Mother and Daddy felt that they had been taken advantage of in order for their nephew to have gainful employment. Although Daddy was angry and bitter, he chose not to pursue the matter through the courts. Instead, he took his savings and bought a furniture store. In not-so-subtle spite, he added a floral business to give his brother and nephew a little competition. We lived upstairs over the store and I felt as secure as any child could feel.

It made up for my lack of siblings when I played with cousins, neighbors and the children of customers. Hide and seek was a favorite game when we visited cousins in the country. The hiding places were so carefully chosen and well hidden that it took hours for all of us to be found. As we community children grew older, we played croquet, badminton and the card game Rook. Adults often joined in the games with us.

Hazard was divided into three communities: Lothair, Walkertown, and Wabco. Each was identifiable by its distinct social strata. My family lived in Walkertown, the most affluent of the three, although we were of average financial means for that area of the state. The letterhead for my father's furniture store read "Engle Furniture Company, Inc.—OUT OF THE HIGH RENT DISTRICT." Each community had its own elementary school, but the few thousand residents that made up the entire town knew each other, and were friends for the most part. There was only one consolidated high school into which three elementary schools merged. Surprisingly, there was not a noticeable problem with cliques.

My mother took great pains to see that I was not prejudiced toward those of other religions, races, or social strata. But when a stranger came to the area, it was quite some time before full trust was extended. Once that trust was earned, however, no more loyal friendships could be found anywhere.

I was eager to begin school in the big two-story building for grades one through eight. A major challenge on the school playground was to run fast enough to beat out everyone else to the best swing available. Nearly all young children enjoy the euphoria of swinging. By first grade I had learned to propel the swing back and forth by pumping my legs. Unfortunately, the swings that I encountered in adulthood were involuntary and painfully debilitating. Although I was probably the smallest child in school, I joined right in with the older kids when they played their favorite, "Crack the Whip." I was always placed on the end because it was so much fun for the bigger kids to swing my light little body. Ironically, I never felt fear from swinging so high.

My first grade teacher was gathering us into our daily reading circle one day when I accidentally pulled a chair out from under another child. Mrs. Dixon insisted that I apologize to the little girl. Because I believed an apology would be admitting that I did it on purpose, I refused to do it. After two hours of isolation in the cloak room, I finally decided to say an insincere, "I'm sorry."

My security and happiness were shattered during my first year in school; but dozens of years would pass before I realized the magnitude of the tragedy that befell our family. The furniture business was struggling because daddy purchased too much inventory, and made other bad business decisions. Although I was not aware of the severity of his problem, I was aware that he gave me less and less attention. Many years later I learned that despondency over the business led Daddy to attempt suicide. Fortunately, the family was able to take the gun from him before he could shoot himself.

I often threw tantrums to get my way. Aware of my own manipulative behavior, I felt terrible guilt when a short time after Daddy's first suicide attempt, he tried it again for the second time, and nearly succeeded. This time he thrust the blade of my mother's sewing scissors into his head. The self-inflicted brain injury resulted in partial paralysis and further depression that kept my father institutionalized most of his remaining life. I feared his action was my fault, and I buried the guilt deep within my psyche where it would remain for several decades. My mother did not drive, but she was determined to give me as normal a life as possible under extremely difficult circumstances. Once again, her strong faith sustained her.

Sympathetic relatives over-indulged me with gifts and attention. Spoiled, demanding, and too talkative, I was a worrisome, attention seeking little girl. My mother consistently took me to church and Sunday school, and she also saw to it that I attend church camps and revivals, all of which steered me to seek God at an early age. At nine-years-old, I was walking home from Girl's Auxiliary Camp when I asked Jesus to come into my heart.

Nine was also the age at which I began piano lessons. My mother and aunt had little confidence in my ability to learn piano. I will always be grateful to Mrs. Dobyne who convinced them to allow me to try. She taught me for eight wonderful years. There have been numerous occasions when my ability to play the piano has been an important tool for me. As an adult, I eventually taught piano, incorporating Mrs. Dobyne's confidence building methods, and bestowing love on my own students.

When Mother found herself widowed, she decided to keep the furniture store. Shortly thereafter, her brother convinced her to convert it to a supermarket. He had gained experience in a food market up north and offered to come back to Hazard to help her run the transitioned business. Mother trusted her brother's advice that in the midst of the economic downturn, furniture sales would drastically fall off. Business was booming when Mother left town to attend my wedding in Hawaii. Soon after her return however, she was totally surprised to learn that her business was suddenly and quickly failing. She had no choice but to sell out in order to avoid bankruptcy.

Mother returned to nursing and moved us to a house, still in the Walkertown neighborhood. Daddy came home for brief periods, but he never went out of the house. Surely people in the community knew of his condition, but even relatives avoided discussing the issue. It was almost as if everyone pretended that Daddy didn't exist.

Setting Out With My Life Mate

When I was thirteen-years-old, I came down with rheumatic fever, a serious illness which often damages the heart. I was treated with Penicillin, six weeks of bed rest and five months of home confinement. The doctor also ordered me to stay out of school the entire year which, of course, meant that I would graduate a year later than my classmates. I was seventeen when I elected to drop out a year short of graduation in order to follow my soon-to-be husband who was entering the service.

Most girls who grew up in the mountains of eastern Kentucky married young in those days. One would think that my mother would have been greatly disappointed when I didn't finish high school. On the contrary, she was quite anxious that I marry Karol whom she had come to dearly love. In hindsight, I believe that my mother strongly suspected that I was destined for mental illness like my father and several of his ancestors. She never thought of herself as intelligent or capable despite the fact that she had become a registered nurse. I suspect that she saw me as less mentally competent than average as well. Whether this was low self-esteem or humility on her part, she no doubt sold herself short, and she also wanted to protect me, her only child from failure.

Had I attended high school as a senior, I likely would have had classes under a teacher who was widely known for excessively high expectations. My music teacher was the only person who tried to dissuade me from dropping out of high school to get married. As I have thought about it over the years, I have concluded that Mother couldn't bear the thought of having me suffer further pain from failure, and rejection from teachers and peers. She quite possibly believed that my immature behaviors and inability to control my constant chatter were a reflection on her. I would like to believe that she agonized over the decision before encouraging me to leave school and get married. She knew that Karol loved me and would take care of me.

I didn't need my mother's encouragement to recognize that I wanted nothing more than to marry the young, handsome, brown-eyed Karol Perkins some day. Karol, a local boy, didn't put up much resistance. My over-protected, pampered upbringing helped me hone the skills that I needed to get what I wanted. I left Karol little chance to escape even had he wanted to.

Karol had a very different upbringing than I. He had been only eighteen-months-old when his father died. His mother abandoned all four of her children when they were very young. Relatives immediately took the children in and cared for them. Karol's aunt and Uncle, Ivra and Russell Osborne, brought him into their home and loved him as if he were their own. However, when he grew older, his mother came back into his life. He had just returned from a visit with her when we had our first date. I was fifteen. He wore yellow canvas shoes and three-dollar jeans. I wore a seventy-five-dollar dress.

While Karol's family had moderate means, they had only slightly less financial resources than my family had. So when I learned that they worried that Karol was dating a girl outside of his social class, I was stunned. In fact they dubbed me "The Uptown Girl." My mother had accumulated a substantial amount of money by this time, but we surely were not wealthy.

Karol borrowed his Uncle's 1946 Dodge truck in which he drove us on our first date. We went to a drive-in restaurant for hot dogs and giggled uncontrollably at something, but for the life of me, I can't remember what had seemed so funny. It probably was a simple case of nervous giggles. We had only four dates before Karol left to serve in the United States Navy, but we wrote letters to each other every single day.

My mother wholly approved of my relationship with Karol, and it was her idea to accompany me on a Christmas visit to his naval base. We were set to go when we learned that Karol would not be allowed off duty status during the holidays, so we didn't make the trip. He had managed to save up about three-hundred-dollars, some of which he used to buy an engagement ring for me. Since his plan to give me the ring at Christmas was thwarted, he sent it to me through the mail. It arrived in February, 1952. That same year, on July 7, we were married in Oahu, Hawaii where he was stationed.

For me, our year and a half in Hawaii seemed like a wonderful fairy tale. We were constantly on the go with friends. Ball games, stock car races and sunbathing on nearby Waikiki beach were great fun. All of the places that we frequented were within walking distance of our living quarters, and we often invited Karol's sailor buddies to meals in our home. Despite my fair skin, my body was tanned to perfection and my strawberry blond hair became even more blond.

I quickly joined a little Baptist church in Hawaii because church had always been an important part of my life while I was growing up in Kentucky. Karol later joined the church as well. I especially enjoyed meeting people from all over the world. As a child I had sung, *"Jesus loves the little children, all the children of the world, red and yellow, black and white, they are precious in His sight . . ."* I still firmly believe that Jesus indeed loves all of His children equally, regardless of race, color, or ethnic background. This sweet and simple truth forms the basis for many of my most meaningful interpersonal relationships today. A Chinese woman and an African-American woman were my best friends in Hawaii. The year and a half that we were stationed there was one of the happiest periods of my life. It was marred only by the news that my daddy passed away during that period, and I was unable to attend his funeral. As a result, feelings of additional guilt were internalized.

Karol was transferred from Hawaii to a ship in San Diego, and I moved back home to Hazard to await the birth of our first baby. On my nineteenth birthday, I gave birth to a precious baby girl and we named her Karol Ann after both of us. When she was three months old, we joined her proud daddy in San Diego, where we remained for yet another year and a half until Karol's service ended. Once again we returned to Hazard.

Young, energetic and idealistic, in 1961, I taught missions to a Girls' Auxiliary group, a part of my church. Each month they learned about local, national, or global missions. Once our group packed a picnic lunch and climbed to the top of a mountain in Hazard. I told them to observe God's beautiful creation from that vantage point. I wanted them to realize that the same creator of this magnificent beauty also made each of us in His own image. I also wanted them to know that our creator God loves each of us equally, and He loves us just as we are. Then I encouraged them to share this truth with others.

My prayers were that God would call at least one of those girls to the mission field. I confess that, at that time, I was prideful of my own missionary zeal. Of course I could never have imagined that I soon would become mired in spiritual darkness which I was unable to control or escape from for many years. Little did I know when I prayed for God to send one of those young girls to the mission field, he would call me to tell the world about Jesus when I reached the ripe old age of seventy-five. While he didn't call me to a foreign land, he called me to reach all who read this small book.

As you read further you will learn more about my journey with Christ. I have assurance that He never fails to keep His promises. He loves us, and He provides for us regardless of our physical, mental or emotional state. He makes no distinction in gender, race, creed or color. He had a plan for every life that He created before the time of our conception. Unfortunately, some reject His plan and attempt to follow their own plan. Too many allow the world to influence who they become. Because God is patient, and full of mercy and grace, all of us can turn and follow Him regardless of the mess we may have made of our lives.[3]

Not long after Karol was released from service and returned to Hazard, he began preparing for a barbering career. We moved to Louisville where he enrolled in barber school. Our second daughter, Debbie was born while we lived there. The adage, "love is blind" was certainly true in our case. Before our marriage, Karol and I never talked about our expectations of each other, but that isn't to say that we had none. As we settled in to work and child-rearing responsibilities, our differences became more exposed. I had no idea that he thought I should like guns, learn to shoot them, and bait my own fish hook. He had no idea that I couldn't cook, keep house or garden. As the years passed, we learned to accept each other's limitations and to compromise. My motto became, "Don't let the sun go down on your wrath."[4]

When barber school was behind him, Karol opened a little barber shop on Main Street in Hazard and began practicing his trade. My widowed mother, a nurse, lived with us at that time, and I stayed busy at home with the children. We entertained friends and neighbors frequently and my husband bought a boat. He loved water recreation, and we spent many hours on a nearby lake. I worked hard to master the skill of water skiing, exerting as much energy screaming as skiing. Of course, each time I opened my mouth to scream, I swallowed a good measure of lake water.

The Honeymoon Ended

When both my husband and my mother left for their jobs each day, I began to experience regret that I was unqualified for gainful employment. I realized that my children would not need me at home forever. Karol suggested that I take the High School Equivalency Test through the General Education Program, but I rejected that course of action for the time being, and sought training as a beautician instead. I was soon accepted at a school in Lexington, which was too far away for daily commutes. My supportive husband found someone to take over his barber shop; sold our boat; rented out our house; bought a mobile home as temporary housing; and found himself a job in Lexington, all within two weeks.

Lexington is quite beautiful. It is surrounded by thoroughbred horse farms, and is known as the Horse Capital of the World. Rolling fields covered with bluegrass are outlined by board fences, usually painted white, but sometimes black. Some fences are built of stone and date back to the 1800s. Horse barns are often more luxurious than the average family residence. A view of the city and surrounding farms from the air is a spectacular sight. Those of us who live here sometimes take the beauty of this place for granted, but when we go away for awhile and come back, we realize that it is one of the prettiest places in this country.

Even before I had completed beautician school we decided to sell our house in Hazard and put down roots in Lexington. We settled into a church, bought another boat, and added a camper to our recreation equipment. Our girls were happy. Beautician school was another story however. Self-doubt set in, and I was excessively fearful of making mistakes that could draw a reprimand from my instructors. The instructors, as well as the other students, enjoyed watching me work in a state of anxiety.

My work station was located by the front desk in view of the entire group of students. The first haircut that I attempted was quite an enjoyable performance for them, but a nightmare for me. I managed to part and section the hair as I had been taught. When it came time to actually cut the hair, I simply slid the scissors across the hair without cutting it at all. I did this all across my client's head before, to my great embarrassment, I looked down to see that no hair had fallen to the floor. I give myself credit for not throwing down my scissors and giving up. I persevered and actually cut the hair successfully on my second try. All the while I endured the laughter of my fellow students and my instructors as well.

Later I made a more serious mistake. I applied a color rinse and a dandruff rinse at the same time. Once I had done it, I asked an instructor to tell me if the procedure was correct. She gasped, "Oh no: that can turn the hair green!" I didn't tell her that the procedure had already been completed. Fortunately, the woman's hair retained its intended color. Eventually I loosened up enough to confide the mistake to another student and we broke up in laughter. It is true that laughter is good for the soul, but only if it isn't at the expense of someone else. For a while then, I overcame my anxiety and fear of rejection.

At twenty-seven-years-old, I was a newly graduated beautician looking for a job. The city was saturated with beauticians, and I was turned down again and again. The more I searched for work, the more dejected I became. Of course my lack of confidence was apparent to prospective employers. I was actually shocked when I was hired by a lady who ran a one-woman salon. She asked me to begin work the very next day. She later admitted to me that I was so funny that she seriously doubted that I would show up for work. At least she didn't say that she thought I was crazy. I never missed a day in the four years that I worked for her.

During my last year at the beauty shop, I developed many anxieties. It became harder and harder for me to make a decision. When I could not find an understanding listener, I developed resentments, anger and sadness. I took my perceived troubles to work with me and burdened my clients endlessly. I was indecisive as to whether my daughters were still young enough to need baby sitters. Or, I wondered if it was fair to allow my mother to help out with them. One of my daughters told me that I was so manic at one point that I was wielding one of my husband's guns and she had to take it from my hand. I do not recall this incident, but it happened before I had been diagnosed as bipolar.

I bleached my own hair and my neck turned red from the chemicals. That is not unusual and I had often seen it happen. Yet, I panicked and saw a doctor who assured me that the condition was not a serious problem and was temporary. I dwelled on our Hawaiian experience as if nobody but me had ever had the privilege of living there. In actuality, I was yearning to return to the happiest days of my life. It became more and more difficult to function at work and at home.

Finally, a client convinced me to see a doctor about my extreme anxiety. She even recommended a specific doctor. I told the doctor that I was suffering from mere nervousness. He performed a Pap smear and checked my estrogen level. A few days later he called to tell me that he would administer an injection of estrogen and prescribe birth control pills. Continuing on a downward spiral, I became more and more anxious.

My husband thought that a vacation would possibly help, so we set out on a family camping trip to Florida. We also invited friends along who owned their own camper. We traveled separately, but in tandem. Well before the vacation was due to end, I became so lifeless that we had to return home. Our friends were driving behind us when Karol was distracted by my constant talking and missed a turn. Our friends followed. We drove many miles out of the way on the winding mountain road. Even had there been a GPS available to us back then, my incessant banter would have drowned out its verbal directions. Karol likely would also have missed seeing directions on a small screen due to my persistent, loud, arm-flinging tirade. He must have been dangerously stressed himself, and I was so frustrated and overwrought by our predicament that the first time the truck stopped, I jumped out and tore the road map into shreds.

The summer wore on and my depression deepened. I perceived myself as having insurmountable problems. I felt sad, empty, worthless, helpless and hopeless. Finally, I shared some of my feelings with the doctor who was monitoring my hormone levels. He said, "It sounds to me as if you are at the bottom end of a totem pole." At his recommendation, I scheduled an appointment with a psychiatrist.

I attempted to pour out my whole life history in one hour on that first visit. On the second visit, I redoubled my efforts to convince the doctor that my worries were legitimate and overwhelming. He asked me to bring my husband with me on the third visit. Karol did go with me, although somewhat reluctantly. When the session ended, the doctor told me that

Karol was on my side. He continued extolling my husband's virtues saying, "Karol is a fun-loving person who is good for you." Apparently the doctor thought a little marriage counseling would do the trick. He ended by admonishing me for being "simply too serious." I felt even more defeated and two weeks later I chose to quit my job.

A Cry For Help

The Thanksgiving holidays fell the week after I left my job at the beauty shop. I phoned my mother to tell her that I did not feel up to the trip to Hazard where all of our relatives traditionally gathered. My mother's voice revealed her keen disappointment. Nevertheless, I prepared for a quiet holiday at home with my immediate family. Then, a well-meaning relative called early Thanksgiving morning to see if perhaps we would change our minds and come to Hazard after all. I read more into the phone call than was intended.

I hung up the phone with overwhelming feelings of guilt and inadequacy. Crying uncontrollably, I tried to explain to Karol the agony that I felt. The more I tried to express my feelings, the more incoherent I became. I could see how my behavior was painful for Karol, and I didn't want to see him hurt by my dysfunction, but I just couldn't cope anymore. Routine incidents were often major disturbances for me. My frustration mounted because I was unable to convince others that my feelings were real.

Being at home alone all day seemed to heighten my despair. I would sit or stand for hours, just staring—completely unaware of the activities around me. Often I felt chilled, so one day I stood too close to the burner on my kitchen range, unaware that I was burning a large hole in my sweater. Karol knew that I was very sick, but he didn't know how to help. Nothing he did seemed to comfort me. He would draw away, busying himself with housework that I was unable to do. After putting in a full day at the barber shop, he would come home to unstop clogged sinks, wash piles of dirty dishes, launder mounds of dirty clothes, shop for groceries, clean the house and prepare dinner for the family.

Meanwhile I quoted scripture which seemed to help me block out the pain. I could tell by their facial expressions, that others were not hearing me say what I intended. One day I decided to phone my minister. His wife answered the phone and she knew immediately by my rapid incoherent babbling that I had a serious problem. I asked her how she knew when Christ was coming. At one point in the conversation, I told her that Karol felt that my mental condition was a private matter, a not-to-be-shared burden. Not wanting to offend my husband, she knew of nothing more to do beyond asking her pastor husband and others in the church to pray that I may find effective psychiatric help.

Later, I again called my minister, and this time he answered the phone himself. I screamed desperate demands that he find a psychiatrist for me. He was to find, not just any psychiatrist, but one who would address my spiritual needs. Off hand, the minister could not come up with the name of a Christian psychiatrist, but he promised to make a few phone calls and get back with me. He was good to his word, and set up an appointment for me with a Christian doctor. I learned that he knew nothing about the doctor's competence. The appointment was made for the very next afternoon which happened to be my oldest daughter's thirteenth birthday.

I don't recall Karol Ann complaining, although she had to make her own birthday cake. Both of my girls seemed (to me at least) to roll with the punches. They were busy with their friends and seemed to adapt to having a mother who was dysfunctional more often than not. Sometimes I would start to prepare dinner and couldn't finish it. The girls would jump right in and complete the meal preparation without a word being spoken. Recently one of the girls told me that they could tell when I was entering a manic episode because of my incoherent speech. When I couldn't make myself understood, they likened my behavior to that of a toddler having a temper tantrum in an effort to get its way. During those times, they coped by putting as much space between us as they possibly could. They realized that I was ill, so they tried to make the best of the situation.

My First Hospitalization

The doctor's office exuded more than mere unfamiliarity. I was absolutely terrified. Pictures on the magazine covers seemed to reach out in an effort to ensnare me. The print was unreadable and threatening. When the doctor was ready to see me, I had curled up in a fetal position in my husband's lap. Immediately the doctor recognized that I needed to be hospitalized. She attempted to admit me that afternoon, but was unable to find a bed for me for two more days.

Meanwhile the doctor prescribed medication which would get me through until I could get into the hospital for a comprehensive examination. As she explained the new prescription to me, she talked to me as if talking to a child. "The medicine is like a hamburger," she said. "A plain hamburger is like the pill you've been taking. You need more than one pill, so I'm adding other medicine just as you add lettuce and tomato to make your hamburger better." The next day was my thirty-first birthday and I slept right through it.

I weighed eighty-five pounds when I was admitted to the hospital on a Sunday morning. Others have described the terror on my face, and my tousled hair as a "wild-woman-look," not that it made me feel better to know that, but at that time I simply didn't care about how I looked. Mainly I feared electroshock treatments, and I was convinced that my bed was wired to shock me at any moment. Also, I was terrified when I went to the bathroom that its walls would burst into flames. Doctors and nurses patiently observed me and administered tests to determine the best course of treatment. It was determined that medication was all that was necessary.

Actually, I was told: "This is your only hope." Even though I had been diagnosed as bipolar, psychotherapy was not considered.

I was released from the hospital one week from the time I entered. My children were then eleven and thirteen. Within a week of my release, I began accepting beginning piano students in my home. It was good for my self-esteem to have the young students look up to me. I felt no stress or pressure whatsoever from them. I truly enjoyed the times when my daughters invited their friends to come home with them after school. Having kids around seemed to elevate my moods when they needed boosting. The fact that I knew where my own children were also lessened my worry about their security. There would be enough cause to worry about them later when they were old enough to go out on car dates.

Both girls were popular, but there was a fair amount of sibling rivalry between them. They managed amazingly well to maintain normal and healthy peer relationships, despite the fact that I was hospitalized several more times during their teenage and young adult years. Of course, I was not always in a depressed state, but seldom were my moods normal. Often I soared too high. During those manic periods I sought unrealistic goals, or I would laugh excessively. My children became accustomed to dealing with my inconsistent behavior. I may have laughed heartily at something one of them said one day, but the very next day, I would find that same statement totally unacceptable.

Karol Ann and Debbie were simply told that I was sick and that they needed to understand that I couldn't help being sick. They seemed to instinctively know that they were expected to accept our family situation and make the best of it. Neither of them complained. Both held great respect for my mother. Mother's presence in our home provided a built-in, stable role model. Her example of accepting, without complaint, those things which can not be changed made a lasting impression on her grandchildren. Later, her great granddaughter, Karol Marie wrote a paper for a school project in which she told of the impact her great grandmother Hallie Engle's life had on her own. Mother was ninety-seven-years-old at the time. Excerpts from that paper follow:

> *"She [my great grandmother] has known the life of many by living so many years and experiencing two world wars, the great depression, and family ... She has an efficient perception of reality ... She has seen the best and the worst aspects of the world we live in today and all that has affected us during the past ninety-seven-years. ... She lives with simplicity and*

nature . . . She used to catch her own fish to eat and to feed her house full of cats . . . She is her own person who can not be changed by others . . . she is a very compassionate person when it comes to life and people. She would cut off her leg to help you in any situation . . . When she hugs you, you know that she loves you more than words can express . . . She believes firmly in equality and free will to do what you wish . . . She looks at all people as the same without prejudging them. Hallie is a very happy person, smiling all the time and occasionally cracking a joke or two. She knows when life calls for a little comedy . . . She never changes herself for anyone, nor does she expect others to change for her. She is a person very content with life and all of creation . . . I would like to follow in her footsteps someday to achieve utter happiness."[5]

Mental illness is less of a stigma today, yet much remains to be done. Knowing that many families are torn apart when one of its members is mentally ill, Dr. Angeline J. O'Malley wrote in an article for *Christian Social Action*, "People do not understand the mentally ill, and that lack of education produces fear and stigma. Churches in particular need to avail themselves in a major way to helping the mentally ill and their families, since this is most often the first place families turn for help. Too many have been shunned and ignored." Dr. O'Malley further states that few pastors are trained to meet the needs of individuals and families affected by mental illness.[6] I whole-heartedly agree with Dr. O'Malley's assessment.

In Sickness and in Health

Karol joined the Shriners organization when my mood swings were temporarily stabilized with medication. On a big Shrine weekend, we had guests and were planning to attend a luncheon and parade. As we were leaving the house to attend the luncheon, I was like an excited child as I hurried down my front steps. Then, I tripped and fell. Although I was unhurt physically, I came apart at the seams. Screaming uncontrollably, I refused to continue with our plans. My visiting friends were stunned by my outburst, and my mother was appalled. I yelled, "The doctor said I can't help myself, only medicine can help me." Needless to say, the good time we had planned was quickly spoiled, and Karol felt embarrassed and humiliated. I later pulled myself together enough to attend the evening activities.

I was never allowed to make many of my own decisions as I was growing up. While my mother probably was trying to protect me from my own bad judgment, by the time I was grown and married, I resented the control she held over me. I felt helpless to do anything about it; even though I understood that likely her fear was that I would inherit the mental illness of my father. She probably thought that by controlling my decisions she could control my fate.

My paternal grandmother and her husband had eight children together. Four of these children suffered mental illness. After my grandfather died of tuberculosis, his widow remarried. One of her second set of seven children suffered mental illness. To my knowledge, none were diagnosed as manic depressive, nor was much known about the condition until more recent years.

My mother could not have known, based on medical knowledge back then, the legitimacy of her fears. However, personal observation of her husband's family history through two generations surely brought her to believe that mental illness was passed down through my grandmother's genes. For whatever reason, she chose to make all decisions regarding my wearing apparel, and I was comfortable with her doing so for many years. I finally recognized that I was much older than most children whose parents had long allowed them to have a voice in their choice of clothing. Throughout my childhood and youth I talked excessively, and I talked loud. I had no discernment in how much was too much. If I thought it, I said it.

At the same time, if I wanted something badly enough, I threw demanding tantrums. It was extremely important to my mother that I was dressed nicer than my peers. We were visiting relatives in Colorado one summer and I fumed throughout most of the trip because I couldn't wear what I wanted to. A taffeta dress on a sightseeing tour seemed like just too much. I was not popular in school, and I believed that it was due to my inappropriate clothes. In hindsight, the reason other kids avoided me was more likely because of my excessive talking.

After we were married, Karol became my mother's cohort in making decisions for me. When my mother came to live with us, it was difficult for me to determine whose instructions to follow. Most of the time, they agreed about what I should and shouldn't do. I almost never offered an opinion of my own. In fact, I came to feel that I was incapable of meaningful thoughts.

Back then I appeared far younger than my age, but only a part of that was due to my short stature. I still looked like a child. At four feet, six inches, I am unable to reach top shelves of closets and cupboards in my home, and I must jump up to get into my bed. I fell once doing that and sustained a large knot on my head. When we realized that I was not seriously hurt, Karol and I had a good laugh over it.

While looking for a way to be more attractive to my husband, I discovered a how-to book on ways a woman can please her husband. One suggestion was to wear a skimpy black nightie, so I shopped for one right away. Unfortunately, my ample bosom makes up for what I lack in height. All of the black nighties that I could find had spaghetti straps. This dilemma can only be understood by top-heavy women whose shoulders bear deep ridges from tiny straps, obviously not designed for weight bearing.

Determined, I took a beautiful pink gown with comfortably wide straps and confidently placed it in my washing machine with a package of black dye. This was my first experience with fabric dying, so I followed package instructions to the letter. The gown came out not black, but a pretty dark charcoal gray. "This should do," I thought, and I wore it to bed that very night. Karol seemed much less impressed than I had hoped. He was greatly surprised however, when the next morning we awoke to find my entire body streaked with black dye. He laughingly assured me that he recognized and appreciated my efforts. We still chuckled years later when we remembered how much I appeared to have just emerged from a coal chute.

Medication was providing stability and confidence sufficient for me to take a part-time job. I began working four hours per day as a candy counter clerk in a large local department store. In addition, I continued teaching my piano students after work. The first two weeks on the job went very well. There is little stress involved with weighing and bagging the candy—then ringing up the sale on a cash register. However, my manager resigned suddenly, and I was expected to take on some of the work that his vacancy created. Anxiety surfaced immediately when I began stocking and taking inventory. I worried that I may sell candy that should be held back for a special sale, or some other equally terrible mistake. Every night I counted candy boxes in my dreams.

It occurred to me that Halloween and Christmas would likely bring extra candy sales, and I decided that I couldn't possibly handle anything more taxing. Also, Karol had become tired of my constant candy-department worries, so he supported my decision to resign. When I approached the manager to give him my decision, he complimented my work and assured me that plenty of help would be available throughout the holidays. I changed my mind and stayed on, but the next three months were a struggle. After Christmas, I did resign, but I felt tremendous turmoil within myself, and I believed that I was a total failure.

Meanwhile, the cost of living skyrocketed. Karol took a second job as an apartment rental agent to supplement our income. The extra work was stressful for him, and I started to worry that he may turn to alcohol. He had detested it in his youth, and refused to frequent Hazard's "Ginny Barns," the local name for bars. I was aware that he recently had imbibed at Shrine functions, so my worries over this issue escalated into an obsession.

My mother no longer lived with us, but one weekend when she and one of Karol's aunts were visiting us, I appealed for their help regarding

Karol's drinking. As I began pouring out my fears, I became increasingly upset. I was literally screaming when Karol came home. Once again, my husband was terribly embarrassed that I "acted up" in front of visiting relatives. His embarrassment turned to anger when he learned the nature of my concern. Indeed, he was drinking on the sly and his guilt, no doubt, added fuel to the fire.

When I realized the extent of Karol's anger, I walked out of the house. It was drizzling rain and I had no idea where to go. I walked around the neighborhood until it began to get late. Finally, I decided to stay in the outside shelter of a church only a few blocks from our house. I had brought my purse with me, but in my haste, I had forgotten my medicine. During the night, I analyzed my hopelessness. I realized that I was helpless to control my own emotions; therefore promises to not lose control again were useless. The psychiatrist who last treated me was no longer available. Also, I considered the expense of psychiatric care through private practice physicians, and determined the cost to be prohibitive.

Finally, I concluded that I should check myself in at Eastern State Hospital, a large, state run mental health facility in Lexington. When morning came, I called a cab to take me there. It wasn't until the cab arrived that I realized that I wasn't carrying enough cash to pay for the fare. The driver could not accept a check, so I couldn't ride. That was probably one relieved cabbie when he realized that he didn't have to transport a little disheveled, obviously distraught woman who had slept out in the dampness. I was undeterred however, and decided to make the trip on foot.

I had walked only a few blocks when it occurred to me to phone my former pastor's wife and explain my dilemma. She had always made a concerted effort to listen to me. I remember little of that conversation, but I revealed enough of my emotional state for her to realize that she needed to call my husband as soon as she hung up the phone with me. Karol had worried about me the entire night and had called neighbors and even the police. The desperation in his voice convinced the police that this was more than a routine domestic quarrel. After all, I had threatened suicide several times, and once I even tried to suffocate myself by placing a plastic bag over my head.

I had continued walking toward the hospital when Karol found me. He jumped out of the car and ran to me with tears streaming down his face. He simply held me for awhile before we drove home. Up to this time,

I had many medication changes and adjustments, several different doctors and many diagnoses, but my misery just wouldn't end.

On another occasion, I awoke on a cold winter morning so terribly discouraged that again, suicide seemed the only answer. I had recently read about a local man freezing to death and that sounded like the solution to end my misery. I wrote a note to my family and drove myself to a local cemetery. I figured that would be the last place anyone would look for me. After I arrived at the cemetery, I decided I wanted to have my hair shampooed and styled first. I suppose pride in my appearance at death was stronger than it was in life at this point.

As I sat under the hair dryer, thumbing through a magazine, I came upon an article about suicide. I ignored the article's suggestion that one should see a doctor when suicidal thoughts persist. But rather than returning to the cemetery after leaving the hair salon, I went home and cleaned the house. Still extremely depressed, I went out and bought a book on the subject of unconditional love. I sat in a restaurant reading until nine o'clock that night. Finally, I felt calm enough to go home.

I had completely forgotten about the note that I left my family that morning. My husband had found it and, of course, took it seriously. He had called my family and my doctor, and all of them felt there was little hope that they would find me before it was too late. I was extremely embarrassed when I realized how much I had alarmed them. I was crying for help and hadn't really wanted to die. I believe that delaying what I had set out to do was an indication that I was biding time for someone to rescue me. I made a concentrated effort after that episode to avoid stressful situations and to slow my daily routine. A new medication soon alleviated my depression, and once again I was back on the road to wellness.

Even when I had progressed beyond suicidal tendencies, I sometimes felt that having a terminal illness might be preferable to enduring painful psychotherapy, apprehension, anxiety, depression and worry. At times I had difficulty distinguishing reality. One such time was when I joined friends at my church to view a video by Christian motivational speaker and comedian, Zig Zigler. Suddenly, I thought I was the person that everyone was laughing at. In my mind, I had turned comedienne. The confusion came and went throughout the entire presentation.

I understood that for me to reach the point of living a meaningful life I must develop more discipline than I felt was possible for me. At the onset of my illness, a doctor told me that my husband would likely seek a divorce. I thank God that Karol never once indicated a desire to end our marriage. Of course, he was frustrated and sometimes angry with me, but I could never have asked for a more loyal partner.

Sustaining Faith

Jesus has been my personal friend since I was very young. I had always gone to Sunday school, Bible School, and summer church camp. When a revival meeting was held, we never missed. The custom when I was growing up was for families of the church to take turns feeding visiting ministers and missionaries. My mother was always eager to open our home to guests, but she was in her element when she was "having the preachers."

I participated three years in a mission Sunday school at a coal mining camp. I played the piano and sometimes sang solos. Still a mere child, at the conclusion of the summer church camp one evening, I began the walk home. My young heart was definitely stirred when I stopped on a little foot bridge and pondered the decision that I knew I must make. I wanted all that God had for me. I had learned the Bible teaching that God's love, mercy and grace are free for the asking. But I had also learned, and believed as true, His requirement that we acknowledge our sinfulness. Yes, my selfishness, jealousy and tantrums were sin, and I had come to recognize that. I knew too, that after we acknowledge sin in our lives, He wants us to ask Him to forgive us.

Most of all, God wants us to invite Him to come into our lives. Only then can we experience all that He has for us. I definitely wanted all that He had for me. I already knew that once we recognize Him as our Lord and Savior He wants us to profess our faith in Him and also to acknowledge that profession before others such as a church body, or a pastor -- at least before another individual who believes in Him. I chose to make my public confession and profession before my church on the very next Sunday morning.

For several years, I committed favorite scripture verses to memory. Two of my favorites are: "God is our refuge and strength, an ever-present help in trouble;"[7] and "Be still and know that I am God . . ."[8] When I was about sixteen-years-old, my voice teacher taught me to sing a beloved hymn, "The Love of God," which quickly became my favorite and remains so today. I share the lyrics here because they were written in an attempt to describe God's magnificent love. I myself know that His love is every bit as tall, deep, and wide as the song describes, yet His love is so much more than any hymn writer could ever capture. The song itself acknowledges that fact.

How the three-verse hymn came to be written, and how I came to love it so much will be apparent as the hymn's story unfolds here:

THE LOVE OF GOD

The love of God is greater far, than tongue or pen can ever tell;
It goes beyond the highest star, and reaches to the lowest hell;
The guilty pair, bowed down with care, God gave His Son to win;
His erring child He reconciled, and pardoned from his sin.
CHORUS:
O love of God, how rich and pure!
How measureless and strong!
It shall for evermore endure
The saints' and angels' song.

When years of time shall pass away, and earthly thrones and kingdoms fall,
When men, who here refuse to pray, on rocks and hills and mountains call,
God's love so sure, shall still endure, all measureless and strong;
Redeeming grace to Adam's race - the saints' and angels' song.

Could we with ink the ocean fill, and were the skies of parchment made,
Were every stalk on earth a quill, and every man a scribe by trade,
To write the love of God above would drain the ocean dry.
Nor could the scroll contain the whole, though stretched from sky to sky.[9]

Frederick M. Lehman, a Gentile songwriter authored the first two stanzas in 1917 after he couldn't forget having heard a camp meeting preacher around 1898 quote the words which became the inspiration, and actually the third stanza. Lehman said, "The profound depths of the four lines moved me to want to preserve the words for future generations." Finally, while taking a break from hard manual labor one day, Lehman picked up a small piece of scrap paper, sat on an empty lemon box pushed against the wall, and with a stub pencil added the first two stanzas and chorus of the song. He had, by this time, learned that the words which had so moved him as they were quoted by the preacher thirty-one-years earlier, actually had been found penciled on the wall of a patient's room in an insane asylum. The general opinion was that the inmate had written the epic in moments of sanity.

Eventually it became known that these words originated in an ancient Jewish poem, *Hadamut*, composed in the Aramaic language in the year 1096. The poem had ninety couplets. The four lines of the third stanza of the hymn must have spoken to the patient who recorded it on the wall of his asylum cell centuries later. It had gone through a slight adaptation from the original composition by Rabbi Mayer, son of Isaac Nehorai, who was a cantor in the city of Worms, Germany.[10]

I see strong irony, or maybe even divine guidance, in that Lehman's inspiration for writing "The Love of God" came from a short stanza of a German Rabbi's poem. The four lines were shared by a preacher at a camp meeting in a mid-western state over 800 years later. A composer happened to hear the preacher as he shared the words that day. Nearly two decades after hearing them, the composer had never forgotten the power of those few words. In 1917, Joseph Lehman added two additional stanzas; then set the three-stanza hymn to music. Eventually, it made its way into the hymnal of my little Baptist church in Hazard, Kentucky. Throughout my life, the words of the song have served as a powerful reminder to me that all people everywhere, no matter how difficult and seemingly hopeless their circumstance, can be comforted in knowing that God's love is abundantly sufficient. Upon learning the hymn's history, I felt further affirmed of my long-held belief that God's children all around the world are all connected through Him.

Much of my adult life was too chaotic to establish a deeper relationship with God beyond the faith of my childhood and young adult years. Yet that mustard-seed faith, first proclaimed on the little Perry County, Kentucky foot bridge, sustained me during the nearly twenty-five years of struggling to attain mental stability. I tried to identify with the Apostle Paul's thorn in the flesh,[11] yet Paul could glorify God despite the thorn. I had the desire to witness for Christ, but I was incapable of doing so. I continued to attend church, even during some of my worst episodes. I did however, refrain from participating in small groups where I might be expected to share anything of my personal life.

Another benefit of my restricted involvement was the protection it provided from my becoming upset with conversation of others. I was aware that I talked far too much myself, but I couldn't seem to help it. I yearned to be understood, but my thoughts raced ahead much faster than I could articulate them. My mind was simply out of control rendering my speech incoherent.

I prayed often that God would send help for me. Deep within myself I knew that the only way that I would be delivered from my misery was through Christ my Lord. During one brief period I sang in the church choir. As I joined in the singing of the great old hymns of assurance, I looked out over the congregation and sincerely felt that God cared for everyone there except me. Once the choir was practicing for a Christmas cantata in an area of the church near where a drama group was practicing. I became caught up in watching the play practice, but the more I watched, the more obscure the play's meaning seemed to me. Suddenly I was terribly frightened and confused. I jumped up and attempted to direct the choir. A friend escorted me out and called my doctor. The doctor convinced me to leave the choir for a while.

There were many times when I felt isolated from the church. My manic episodes frightened some so much that I was ostracized. A few implied that good Christians don't become mentally ill. I now realize that being in the body of Christ doesn't automatically make people knowledgeable and compassionate. While many church members and clergy alike are untrained in how to minister to the mentally ill, many do care, and they pray for those of us in their midst who need it. Even when I felt alone and uncared for, I sang the songs with words that had comforted me during my childhood and youth.

A scripture that came to my mind often was, "I came that they might have life, and might have it more abundantly."[12] During one hospital stay, I had been put in isolation and strapped down. I was given the name of the nurse in charge as each shift changed. My instructions were to call the nurse's name if I needed anything. I was terribly afraid that I wouldn't be able to remember the correct name when I needed to. A few days before that I had overheard a staff member discussing her belief in the Holy Trinity. I too hold a strong belief in the Trinity. Thereafter, when I needed to summon a nurse I would scream, "God the Father, God the Son, and God the Holy Spirit." Then the name of the nurse always came to my mind. I was removed from isolation at the end of three days, but it seemed as if I had been there for an eternity. Some time during the remaining weeks of that hospital stay, I received an encouraging message. Karol's aunt had been praying for me. She woke up suddenly one night and saw a distinct, but tiny light far in the distance. She was certain that the light represented me, and she felt God's strong assurance that I would eventually be healed. I did not feel God's love and peace, but I did depend on His Word which was hidden in my heart. I cried out to Him over and over begging Him to send a Christian person who would listen as I bared my inner-most soul.

Ann as a happy two-year-old

Five-year-old Ann with her father

Ann's future husband Karol at eighteen

Ann at fifteen

Ann on her wedding day in Hawaii

Ann rocking client's baby in her daycare

Despair to Joy

Ann's parents Harve and Hallie Engle

Happy newlyweds Ann and Karol Perkins

Perkins family portrait

Ann's memorable pony ride in Texas

A Breakthrough At Last

A friend, in casual conversation, mentioned hearing of a Christian psychiatrist with an impressive reputation. She gave me the doctor's name and then added, "I'm told his office walls are decorated with prayers and scripture plaques. He also prays with his patients." I wanted to leap for joy. Indeed, a Christian psychiatrist, and a bold one at that, was practicing right here in Lexington. I filed away the doctor's name, unaware that I would need to retrieve it very soon.

When I first saw Dr. John, as I came to call him, I had already been admitted to a hospital psychiatric ward. The only thing that I recall about our first encounter is the unusual prescription-like note that he asked me to take home. He had written my name, and the date, February 9, 1979. Then, below that, he wrote: "Say at least 5 times daily while looking in mirror:

GOD LOVES ME
MY HUSBAND, MY DAUGHTERS, AND DR. FREER LOVE ME
I LOVE ME, OR I'M TRYING TO

I was perplexed by the last item. I had been taught to love others, but I equated self-love with self-centeredness. Why was I being asked to love myself? Was this not a contradiction? I pushed the entire confusing idea aside. It was several more months before I mustered courage to entertain the idea of loving myself.

I was in a manic state when I first saw Dr. John. I quoted scripture most of the time. Although I understood myself perfectly, others heard only loud, fast, unintelligible ranting. For a while, I was afraid of all the male patients in the hospital. I realized that there was no real basis for my fear, therefore, I chose not to report it to the hospital staff. I simply stayed in my room.

Finally, I grew weary that my self-imposed isolation was keeping me from activities that were available in the patient's day room. I developed a plan. I marched into the day room, headed straight for the piano, and began playing classical music. My thought was that my choice of music would not be to the men's liking. As I had hoped, it worked. All of the men fled the room, and most of the women did too. I felt so very clever. It didn't occur to me at the time that my playing was probably as off key as my speech was rambling. Any type of music that I may have chosen to play would likely have cleared the room.

People in a manic state often sleep little. I was no exception. I had kept my roommate awake for three nights before I was finally placed in isolation. I hated being in the room alone; and the time that I spent there dragged unmercifully. I was allowed to leave the room for meals but one day I refused to return. Although I don't remember the incident, I am told that I locked both my arms and legs across the door frame and held on with supernatural strength. It took three men to pry me loose and get me back inside the room.

During that period I dreamed of a visit by dead relatives including my father. All of them had been mentally ill. In the dream, one person spoke to me and told me to hold on tight. When I was released from seclusion, I no longer feared men, but I retained some unusual behaviors which often were triggered by the power of suggestion. A nurse mentioned the fact that my feet were small. Immediately after that, I encountered a male nurse outside the door of my room. His shoes were at least size thirteen. I stared at my size four feet, then back at his. I was glued to the spot. The contrast absolutely perplexed me. Soon patients and staff alike gathered to watch me watch our two pairs of feet.

Finally my condition stabilized and I was released from the hospital. Dr. John set a follow-up office appointment with me. Although I strongly sensed God's hand in bringing this doctor to me, I still expected to be dismissed from the hospital and sent home with medicine and maybe the name of another psychiatrist. When I realized that Dr. John actually wanted to retain me as a patient, I was elated. He had actually chosen me.

I was apprehensive but excited when I went for the first office visit. Just as I had been told, the office walls reflected the doctor's Christian faith. The first thing to catch my eye was a ribbon of nine plaques. A fruit of the spirit was on each: love, joy, peace, patience, kindness, goodness, faithfulness, gentleness, and self control.[13]

Dr. John asked me to choose the one fruit that I most wanted to claim for myself. Without hesitation, I chose peace. We established an initial schedule of thirty minutes each week. Dr. John immediately dispelled any notion that I may see him as God. He loaded me down with reading material and suggested daily Bible study and prayer. E. Stanley Jones' *How to be a transformed person* and *Abundant Living* were two books that greatly encouraged me.

It was apparent to Dr. John and to me also by that time, that I must remain on medicine. In addition, I needed much deep inward delving. Dr. John asked me to write down any thoughts and feelings that I could about my life experiences from childhood to the present. I wrote of positive experiences almost exclusively. This was of course inconsistent with the terrible guilt and anger that I was holding within myself. Dr. John instantly saw through the mask.

We had barely begun psychotherapy when an emergency sent me back to the hospital. Our daughter Debbie was making wedding plans, and I became simply overwhelmed by it all. Karol saw the pattern developing; therefore, he was anticipating another hospitalization. A suggestion that I may want to consider entering the much more affordable Eastern State Hospital infuriated me. However, that was to be my third hospitalization within that year, and the costs had already mounted significantly. I chose to express my anger by swallowing thirty aspirin.

Karol was discouraged and impatient with my lack of progress. I had not seriously wanted to die, but I had wanted to make a statement about the pain I was feeling. Once the aspirin were pumped from my irritated stomach, Dr. John released me from the hospital. As we prepared to leave for home, we were given a heavy dose of straight talk to impress upon us the importance of following his professional advice. We understood that heeding his advice was my only hope. Karol then began counseling with Dr. John himself, mainly to learn how to best help me. He also needed help to endure the turbulence, and unpredictability of my mental state.

Debbie's wedding did take place as planned. Just prior to her marriage, I wrote a letter to her future husband. It was dated October, 1982. Our son-in-law, Scott, recently sent me a copy of the letter that he had kept more than twenty years. I was pleased to find that within the long-forgotten letter, I had expressed delight at having him as our future son-in-law. I had also told him of the joy that Debbie had brought us. I wrote, "We trust that she will bring that joy to you." I went on to tell him that Debbie had been a good baby and had smiled most of the time throughout her life. I talked of the happy times when the girls went sledding on the hillside near our house in Hazard, and how, at her kindergarten graduation, Debbie stole the show when she stepped to the edge of the stage and announced, "I love you mommy." I can never forget that moment when my chest nearly burst with pride.

The Great Unraveling

As a young man, Karol had abhorred the thought of alcohol. His uncles had been alcoholics and he wanted no part of the consequences. He had witnessed first hand its ability to destroy families. However, he began to drink socially when he joined the Shrine organization. Soon thereafter, the family began to struggle financially and I had to quit working at the candy counter. Karol took on a second job and the extra work added to his stress. My declining mental state became an overwhelming burden to him.

Most Eastern Kentuckians, back then, brought up their children to believe that sharing family problems was "airing dirty linen;" a practice that should be avoided at all costs. Mental illness, still considered shameful in many circles, was in the dirty linen category. It was not hard to understand why Karol couldn't bring himself to ask for help. Consequently, he began to drink more and more to block out his pain. He reached a point where he simply didn't care that he couldn't stop drinking.

At first he drank only on weekends, but eventually he drank all during the week. Fortunately, his drinking didn't interfere with his ability to work. It did however, create guilt and shame within him, and he withdrew from activities and hobbies that he had previously enjoyed. It was harder for me to accept the fact that he no longer wanted to go out with friends, than the fact that he was harming himself physically. As time went on, the physical damage grew more and more serious. Finally, in 1987, Karol joined Alcoholics Anonymous. At about the same time, I began a concentrated effort to recall everything that I experienced during my childhood as far back as I could remember. Karol was also counseled by Dr. John in an attempt to better understand how he could relate to me. A bit later Dr. John counseled him in how he could refrain from drinking.

Karol successfully refrained from drinking when he attended a *Walk to Emmaus*, a three-day spiritual retreat. When he returned from the retreat, he felt confident that he would no longer need alcohol as a crutch. Unfortunately that confidence was short-lived, but to his credit, Karol soon enrolled in a six-week chemical abuse program where he was assigned a mentor who stayed by his side through the duration of the program. I thank God that, through that program, he did break the habit and never drank again the rest of his life.

As Dr. John continued to counsel me, he insisted on minute detail from my past. I had freely talked about feelings of embarrassment at having to dress inappropriately; feelings of loneliness because I had no siblings; and feelings of inadequacy due to my decision to drop out of high school in order to get married. I told of my beauty school experiences, and other more recent issues, but I omitted a major issue—my father's botched suicide and its consequences.

Starting the process of childhood recall was easy enough. I remembered that my family lived at the head of a "holler" in Flat Woods, Kentucky when I was three or four-years-old. Rip, a teen-aged boy lived with his family at the top of the hill above our house. He often allowed me to accompany him for horseback rides. No doubt about it, Rip was my first love.

My mother carried all of our household water supply from a spring, and she stayed busy canning vegetables from her own vegetable garden. Sometimes she packed a picnic lunch and we spent the day picking berries at the blackberry thicket. She spread a quilt out in an open area for me to sit on where she could keep an eye on me. The biggest danger in that was that poisonous copperhead snakes were common there in the mountains. Fortunately we never were snake-bitten. Sorghum making took place out by the spring every year, and people came from all around. That was one of the year's major social events. For me, licking the sweet sticky molasses from a spoon was as much fun as a little girl could ever want.

I recalled that my father was recovering from tuberculosis when the family moved to San Antonio, Texas. It was hoped that the environment there would speed his recovery. We lived near a big golf course, and I picked up the golf balls that fell outside the fence. While we lived there, we witnessed the biggest snowfall in South Central Texas' history. I bitterly remembered not being allowed to play in the snow because I was sick. I could only watch through the window as all of my little friends frolicked to their hearts' content. One fond memory of living there was riding ponies at an amusement park.

Whether the stay in Texas was responsible or not, my father did recover from TB, and we moved back home to the Kentucky mountains. We lived in an apartment while preparations were made to open a combination furniture store and florist shop. One night while we were asleep, the furnace blew up. I remembered clearly my terrible fear as we ran outdoors in the middle of the night. Fortunately no one was injured.

The business was soon established and, for a while, it provided more financial security than our family had ever known. Unfortunately, my father's mental health began to decline soon thereafter. When I was six-years-old, Daddy attempted suicide, and almost succeeded. I blocked out most of what happened that day for at least six years. I still have not recalled all of it. As I remembered, I had come home from school to learn of the tragedy. My father was paralyzed on one side from the damage he inflicted upon his brain with a blade of my mother's sewing scissors. Of course the brain damage further complicated his existing mental problems. My father was in and out of mental hospitals until his death eleven years later.

Family outings came to an end because my mother didn't drive. I felt totally isolated. Although I hadn't remembered, a review of old report cards confirmed that my grades fell dramatically after my father's suicide attempt. My behavior was always at its worst when visitors came to our home. I usually managed to earn a spanking, and/or was sent to bed early. I taunted one cousin incessantly. One of my uncles complained that my constant loud talking got on his nerves.

My mother continued running the business on her own after Daddy was institutionalized. She found that she must hire live-in help to keep up with the domestic chores. Mother took me along with her to visit Daddy at Eastern State Hospital in Lexington when I was about nine-years-old. I suspect that no one had been available to watch me at home. Since I was still too young to be allowed inside the hospital, my mother left me in the care of a man at the front gate of the hospital grounds. I believe the man may have been a patient who had ground privileges. He stayed near me for a while, but then he wandered off leaving me alone. Of course, I was quite frightened. Finally, a female patient took a seat on the bench next to me and started talking. I became even more frightened. The woman finally left, but I was afraid that she would return, or that someone more threatening would take her place.

I ventured out on my own across the wide expanse of lawn lined with clusters of red brick buildings. I walked toward the building that I believed my mother had entered. There I found an inviting porch swing at the entrance, and sat there to wait. Although I didn't know it, the swing was in view of my father's room, and my mother saw me sitting there waiting. I didn't get to see my daddy that day, but he probably saw me.

Mother's visits to see my father in the hospital depended upon when someone could drive her. Occasionally she took a bus. I was not allowed to enter the hospital to visit Daddy until I was fourteen-years-old. That restriction added confusion and unhappiness to my young life. Once when Mother visited Daddy his condition was so poor that she elected to remove him from the hospital, and bring him home. He screamed all night long, so she took him back to the hospital the very next day.

Once again, we were awakened during the night by neighbors who alerted us to a fire in the store's stockroom adjoining our apartment. Although the neighbors routed us to safety and helped throw our furniture out as a precaution, the fire didn't reach our apartment. We stayed with friends for a few days until minor damages were repaired. The malicious nature of the stock room fire taught me first hand that there are sometimes those who deliberately endanger the lives of innocent people. That lesson has affected my sense of security from then on.

We moved from the apartment over the store to a house when I was about ten-years-old. Soon afterward, Daddy was released from the hospital. I had been taking piano lessons for about a year and I practiced playing Daddy's favorite hymn over and over to perfect it as a welcome home gift. Mother managed to keep him at home for two years during which time he read two classics: *The Robe,* and *The Big Fisherman.* He immersed himself completely in his reading, and for months thereafter, those two books dominated his thoughts and conversation. The only medication that he took during that time was for the control of seizures. He never left the house throughout those two years. I could not understand why we could not be a normal family.

I barely passed sixth grade, but at the end of that school year, my father returned to the hospital never to come home again. The next year I contacted rheumatic fever which prevented me from attending school for a year. Finally, by eighth grade, I became serious about my school work. I attribute this turn mainly to a conscientious male teacher who helped motivate me to study. My confidence began to return, and my grades steadily improved for the next two years.

When I turned fourteen, I finally was allowed to go with my mother inside my father's hospital room. The harsh sound of metal doors being unlocked and relocked set me on edge as we made our way toward the large visiting room. At my mother's insistence, I wore a bright red hat and white gloves. The visiting room was filled with male patients and all of them were staring at me. I was positive that they were staring because they thought my hat looked strange. Daddy was not in the visiting room, so we started toward his room. On the way, I thought of the times the hospital staff had asked my mother to send money to replace clothes that Daddy had ripped apart. His disability left few outlets for him to relieve frustration and anger. I wondered just what state he would be in today. We found him lying on his bed, one of many in a large ward.

He seemed to vaguely recognize us when we first arrived. He teasingly reminded me, "Watch out for the boys." This was his way of acknowledging my budding womanhood. He had slowly regained full use of his extremities, but his awareness was fleeting. An orderly entered the room and Daddy thought he was Earl Clements, a former Kentucky governor. Launching into political rhetoric, my father completely lost touch with reality, and was oblivious to the presence of his wife and daughter. A nurse asked us to leave while the orderly took Daddy away to the bathroom. That was the last time that I saw my father alive. He died four years later at the age of fifty-four while I was living in Hawaii with my new husband.

Memories of my childhood that I could recall were exhausted, but Dr. John astutely recognized that I continued to carry an extraordinary load of guilt and anger. He explained to me that young children often assume guilt for a tragedy for which they have had absolutely no responsibility. Once again, he insisted that I return to the period in my childhood when my father botched his suicide attempt. He specifically asked that I concentrate on the six years from that period forward. I knew that I needed help to successfully bring forth anything meaningful, so I solicited the prayers of my mission group.

The prayers began, and I, pad and pencil in hand, started phoning cousins, aunts, and others to tap their memories. I had a strong sense that God was about to help me unravel an extremely complex tangle. I quickly became discouraged however, when all that the relatives seemed to remember was how terribly spoiled and demanding I had been as a child. Yet, I persevered in the process because I felt driven at this point.

During that intense effort of trying to recall more of my childhood, my mother came to visit. The timing was right to broach the subject with her. I mustered the courage to talk about how terribly shocked I had been to come home from school to see Daddy paralyzed. My mother's head jerked up in obvious surprise. She said, "But Ann, you didn't come home from school to find out, you were at home somewhere that day at the time Daddy stuck those scissors in his head. In fact, you had been eating too many cookies a bit earlier and your daddy scolded you for it. There was no school that day." Where exactly had I been? What did I witness? What had I been doing? Mother didn't know, and to this day, I do not know the answer to those questions.

Trying as hard as I could, I could not then, and I still can't recall anything more of that fateful morning. Whatever I experienced was sufficiently traumatic to cause me to block it out of my mind forever. It now seems inconceivable that I had not discussed this with my mother earlier. Of course, she had no idea that I didn't remember the details just as she did. I was expecting that, with this knowledge, Dr. John would want to end the psychotherapy. I thank God that was not the case. He simply intensified therapy to help me understand that I was in no way responsible for my father's actions. Within two months, I began to experience a new freedom of spirit. Not only was I being freed of false guilt, I was realizing that through God's grace I could forgive all those who had hurt me.

Spiritual Formation

Early in my visits with Doctor John, he advised me to establish daily devotional and prayer time. I dutifully took his advice, but most of my earlier prayer experiences were filled with petitioning God for my own needs. Later, I joined the prayer line at my church. The progression to intercessory prayer was a big step in my growth toward spiritual maturity. Yet another leap forward occurred when I joined a weekly prayer group led by Margaret Therkleson, a well known writer and speaker on the subject of prayer. People come from all over Central Kentucky to pray corporately within this powerful spirit-filled group.

I study the Bible daily and read other inspirational writings. My favorite contemplative author is Thomas Merton, a Trappist Monk. I could relate well to him, especially when I learned of his young-adult years of indecision and discontent. Finally Merton entered the Abby of Gethsemane, near Bardstown, Kentucky. He was a prolific writer who struggled for years to reconcile the monastic life with his vast international experiences and the many friends that he had acquired while attending Cambridge and Columbia Universities.

In his college days, he was a social activist and student of comparative religion. Gethsemane's Abbot refused to allow Merton (renamed Father Lewis by that time) to leave the Abby to research spirituality and social justice issues needed for his writing assignments. Eventually a new Abbot came to Gethsemane and allowed Merton to travel to Asia.

Before his untimely death due to accidental electrocution, Thomas Merton had written 70 books, most on contemplative life, prayer and religious biographies. Near the end of his life he wrote increasingly on social justice, and ecumenical concerns.[14] Merton's concerns have been my concerns from a very early age. His writings are a great resource as I seek solitude and contemplation for my self.

In times when I felt unworthy, I chose Father John Powell's books on unconditional love. I had always known on one level that God loved me, but sometimes my emotions told me that he would give up on me. I hated myself, and cried out in anger and resentment at those who were trying to love me. Then I would panic, fearing that "now they won't love me for sure."

Dr. John did not give up on me, and he accepted me and helped me to work through all of my self-hatred, reassuring me over and over that there is hope. I continue to pray that God will give me the ability to show more unconditional love to others as I have received it, and finally accepted the wonderful experience that had been there all along. While it is always easier to love those who love you, hurting people need love despite what they do or say.

Other writers whose works were helpful to me were Scott Peck and Robert Schuler. My husband, although a believer, eventually stopped going to church. Still, he didn't object to my going, and he actually helped me design and develop a private meditation garden tucked away in our back yard. It provided a time apart from interruptions and distractions of the world. I was truly alone with God in my little outdoor sanctuary. I eventually came to realize that God wanted to stretch me more by having me serve others.

I found a card tucked in my Bible on which the prayer of Jabez was written. I began praying the prayer for myself every day. Jabez asked God to bless him, to enlarge his territory [increase his responsibility], to stay close by him, and to keep him from harm.[15] God granted Jabez what he asked for. Shortly after I began praying the prayer of Jabez for myself, God expanded my territory as well.

I began to visit a nursing home on a regular basis. An elderly woman who was unable to turn herself over in bed, wanted nothing more than to hear the Bible read to her. I gladly accommodated her wish. Once I even took my piano students there to perform their recital for the residents. Another time on Valentines Day, I dressed my seven-year-old granddaughter in a red dress and had her carry a basket filled with funny valentines to give to each resident. I also accompanied a Chaplain as he made his prayer rounds at one of the local Veterans Hospital.

Later, I served as a Pink Lady at Good Samaritan Hospital. My job was to assist people in the ICU waiting room. Another little assignment was to remind the patients of Chapel service times on Sundays. Interaction with nursing home and hospital patients took my focus away from myself and placed it on others who were sick, infirm and often lonely. It was a wonderful feeling to know that I had helped brighten someone else's day.

Successful Transition

My beloved Dr. John had patiently stayed by my side for ten years. His treatment and counsel had slowly but surely brought me from despair to joy. However, in 1990 this outstanding Christian psychiatric professional made the decision to move his practice to Western Kentucky, almost a day's drive from Lexington. He left me with the assurance that another Christian psychiatrist would take me as a patient on his referral. For that I was truly grateful. I knew that it was extremely important for me to be under the care of a competent psychiatrist for monitoring and prescribing the medication that I will require for the rest of my life. Dr. John also left me with this scripture:

> "Finally brothers, whatever is true, whatever is noble, whatever is right, whatever is pure, whatever is lovely, whatever is admirable – if anything is excellent or praiseworthy – think about such things."[16]

When my new psychiatrist, Dr. Bob (assumed name) began seeing me, I immediately felt comfortable and assured of his competence. Although Dr. John had given him massive amounts of data prior to my seeing him, he encouraged me to tell him anything that I thought he would not already be aware of. He particularly wanted to hear how I was currently feeling, and whether I was still plagued by racing thoughts as I once had been. Amazingly, the transition from one doctor to another was almost seamless. Doctor Bob ended our visit with a prayer each time that I saw him for evaluation. I was no longer experiencing mood swings and racing thoughts. Nevertheless, when under stress, I slammed each of my clenched fists to the sides of my head over and over. The force was such that it could possibly have cracked my skull. I couldn't explain why I was doing it.

I recognized this behavior as something that I needed to share with Dr. Bob. His immediate response was, "This has nothing to do with your bipolar disorder. It is from Satan." I was stunned at this response, but I trusted that it was true, and from that day forward the head bashing never occurred again. The incident also served to teach me how Satan had tried to use my mental illness to destroy my peace and joy. Among the things that he surely was responsible for were my previous thoughts of suicide. I knew from my prayer sessions with Margaret Therkleson that we must always be on the alert for Satan's attempt to lead us astray. Our best defense to block him is prayer in the name of Jesus. I learned how to more quickly recognize and resist the enemy through the teachings of New Zealand healing minister, Craig Marsh. He cites dozens of names given to the enemy in the Bible. Each name has a meaning which helps to define the type of attack that the evil one will choose to achieve a specific desired effect. Examples from Marsh's list alert us to Satan's methods which he customizes for optimum impedance to our relationship with God:

- Satan (the adversary) gives power to resist – Desired effect is to cause frustration
- Abaddon (the destroyer) gives power to persecute – Desired effect is intimidation
- Accuser – gives power to condemn – Desired effect is suffocation by condemnation
- Serpent (the deceiver) – power to deceive – Desired effect is to lead us astray
- Devil (the slanderer) – desired effect is to cause separation and division among us
- Lucifer (Beelzebub, which means lord of the flies: known to pollute and defile) – desired effect is infiltration – working from within us to pull things down around us.[17]

"Once we begin to understand how the enemy is attacking us, we can associate it with a tactic of the enemy; we are more able to resist him and defeat him. Christ disarmed the evil rulers, despoiled them of their powers, casting them aside like an outworn garment. Jesus made a public spectacle of them nailing their powers to the cross. We have the victory in the death and resurrection of Jesus."[18]

Now that I recognize how easily my thoughts and behaviors can be manipulated, I am careful to question their source. I am free of worry and fears, and confident that God wants me to have all fruit of the spirit which I had seen listed on my doctor's plaque so many years ago. Dr. Bob continued to monitor me for bipolar symptoms, and when necessary he adjusted my medicine. Occasionally he counseled me if he felt it was needed. He was patient, but straight forward with me, and I was comfortable in telling him things about my past. Occasionally I found myself telling him things that I had totally repressed during my years with Dr. John. The most significant revelation had to do with my relationship with my mother who passed away in 1999, just twelve days shy of her one-hundredth birthday.

My mother was strong spiritually, but also physically and emotionally. She had worked hard all of her life, but in her last years, she suffered financial hardship. She lost her home, and spent her last few years living with her sister in Hazard. She was greatly loved by our entire family. Once I began to openly talk with Dr. Bob about our relationship, he realized, and helped me to realize that Mother's control over me was motivated by her desire to protect me from experiencing painful rejection and failure that she feared I would be exposed to.

Six years from the time I first saw him, Dr. Bob retired. Yet again, I am under the care of another Christian psychiatrist. He only needs to see me twice each year. He is particularly pleased that I no longer have racing thoughts. Best of all, the dramatic mood swings have stopped.

My Own Business

By 1995, I had come to a place of physical and emotional stability. My days were peaceful, contented, and even joyful. However, I was fully aware that I must continue on medication that requires regular monitoring. I also knew that it was important that I maintain low stress levels. Dr. John had suggested several years earlier that rather than working with adults, I could probably do well caring for infants in my home. I became certified by the city to care for up to three infants at a time. I chose to care for babies new-born, to age two.

One room in my home was outfitted with the necessary baby paraphernalia. The most essential furnishing was a nice rocking chair. Parents learned of my service by word-of-mouth, and I was soon operating to capacity. Feeding and nap time for the toddlers varied little. Every baby in my care was rocked and sung to every day. My repertoire varied, but *Jesus Loves Me* was sung daily without fail. I had forgotten parts of many other songs about Jesus, but I sang what I could remember.

A caring neighbor checked in on the babies and me every day. When on rare occasions I needed to be away for something such as a doctor's appointment, the same neighbor was always willing to watch the babies for me. This practice was always communicated to the parents so they could have the option of finding a temporary caregiver on their own, or trusting their babies with my neighbor who they all knew.

At one point I was doing so well that I talked my doctor into allowing me to try going without my medicine. In just a few days I experienced a full-blown manic episode. Parents of my babies were notified, and two days after I resumed the medication, I was able to care for the babies again. I had told all of the parents up-front that I was bipolar, but they knew that I had not had an episode for several years, and none since starting my childcare service. Two of the three sets of parents chose to continue using my services.

Most of those precious babies are grown, married, and have moved on. Although they are scattered far and wide, they are still close to my heart. I pray for each of them still, and also for their families. I recently learned that one of the babies, now twenty-six, plays guitar and leads praise and worship for two different groups in a large Dallas church. While I have lost touch with many of my former babies, I know that one is a lawyer, one is a nurse, one is an engineer and another is president of a successful education resource corporation.

While in my care, I sang to them about Jesus every day. I prayed that the words would penetrate their little hearts and minds and lead them to recognize and love Jesus themselves when they grew older. Setting up a mini-childcare center in my home was low stress, and it turned out to be a good decision which gave me full-time gainful employment and personal fulfillment. The pay was not much, and there were no paid vacations, or health benefits; nevertheless, when I retired in 2003 after 23 years, I knew that childcare had been the most gratifying job that I could have ever hoped for.

More Health Problems

For the most part my physical health had been strong over the years. As it so often happens when women reach middle age, I underwent a minor gynecological surgery under local anesthesia at age 53. There were no complications and recovery was amazingly fast, but five years later, I was diagnosed with diabetes. At the time I was twenty pounds overweight and my doctor felt that the diabetes could be reversed with the proper diet and exercise. Wanting to avoid more medication, I immediately began an exercise regimen.

I arose every morning at 4:00 a.m. and headed to the YMCA to walk the track. This allowed me to be home before the babies arrived. Within a year I had lost a mere ten pounds, and I had not changed my eating habits one iota. Of course, I gained back every bit of the weight quicker than I had lost it. Eventually my doctor placed me on medication to control my blood sugar. Having to control two major health concerns increased my stress.

Treatment for mental illness is expensive and the many years of psychiatric care and medical costs took its toll on our financial situation. Even though we had insurance, we were forced to sell our boat, motor and camper in order to pay the bills. We were fortunate to be able to keep our split-level home in a nice neighborhood. Karol Ann took a job in the restaurant of a major department store when she turned sixteen. Likewise, Debbie began working in another department of the same store as soon as she was old enough. Their income allowed them to have things that we could not otherwise have afforded. They paid for their own cars, and also their own weddings. Debbie even paid for her own college education. Karol

Ann continued working at the department store, and moved up the ranks to a very good position.

Betty, a friend from church was a loyal listener for me during that time. Through our daily phone conversations, she knew almost as much about me as my psychiatrist did. Her patient listening and quiet spiritual counsel was incredibly helpful at a time when I was not yet at a place where I felt that I could depend solely on the Lord. Neither could I afford more frequent counseling sessions. Everyone should have a loyal, selfless friend like Betty to be there just to listen. If one doesn't already have such a friend, I suggest that petitioning God to provide one is in order.

I had driven a large old Cadillac for years, although it was hard for me to see over the steering wheel because I am so short. It was necessary that I pull the seat as far forward as possible, and then sit on a stack of pillows. The boost allowed my feet to reach the accelerator and brake. But when the car finally was worn beyond repair, I had to purchase a new vehicle. I could never seem to position myself well enough to see all that I needed to from the new car. That problem, along with a blinding sun, resulted in my crashing into another vehicle as we entered the intersection simultaneously. The victim was merciful and very grateful that neither of us was injured.

Not long after that accident I fell asleep at the wheel and rear-ended yet another vehicle that had stopped in front of me. Once again, I was fortunate that there were no injuries. I willingly gave up driving altogether at that time. I had been falling asleep at other inappropriate times, and had so little energy that my daughter accompanied me on one of my doctor visits. She sensed that I was over-medicated. The doctor heard her out and substantially decreased one of my prescriptions. It has made a major difference in my daily activity.

Karol's Last Days

Early in the nineties, through intensive counseling, Dr. John helped Karol to cease his alcohol dependency in order to attend a three-day spiritual retreat, the *Walk to Emmaus*. He had a great experience and came home from the event happier than I had ever seen him. He was proud of himself that he had abstained from drinking throughout the three days that he had been away. He felt confident that this was the beginning of his recovery.

Karol was also attending Alcoholics Anonymous meetings which indicated a sincere desire to break his addiction. Unfortunately the stresses of life weakened his resolve and he caved in to the craving. He also had a strong addiction to cigarettes and consequently developed COPD and chronic bronchitis. Eventually he had to retire as a barber and soon required oxygen full-time.

In 2003, our daughters determined that our physical and emotional stress due to loss of income could be substantially alleviated if we sold our house and moved to a retirement facility. They helped us find a very nice two-bedroom apartment in East Lexington. Moving meant leaving a place which held many memories. Some were good, particularly during the last ten years there, but many were terrible. The memories that all of our family would like to forget were the worst years of my illness.

The new residence had every convenience that we could need, and we felt blessed to gain the friendship of other residents, and the great staff in the multi-story facility. I seldom think of the bad times now. An exception is when I see an opportunity to share my personal story. I am on a mission to let others know that recovery from the despair and pain of bipolar disorder is indeed possible.

Despair to Joy

Karol continued to grow more and more weak. He stayed in bed most of the time and finally had to be hospitalized. He was diagnosed with chronic bronchitis. Chest X-rays revealed that he had a mass on his lungs which his doctor felt was surely malignant, but it could not be confirmed without a surgical biopsy. Karol asked that no further diagnostic procedures or treatment be done. His wish was honored. He wanted only to be sent home to live out his final days.

Sadly, Karol still had not given up cigarettes, even though he was on oxygen. Of course, that is extremely dangerous because of the oxygen's flammability. Eventually, when word got to facility managers that he was smoking in the presence of oxygen, they explained to him that unless he immediately ceased smoking on the premises, we would be evicted. Not only was he endangering himself and me, but everyone in the entire building was at risk. Only then did he finally stop the life-long smoking habit.

I was now confined to home most of the time because my terminally ill husband needed me there. During the last months of his life, a service company sent meals to us, helped with house cleaning, provided transportation to our doctors' offices, and even provided a sitter for Karol while they transported me to the grocery store. About a month before Karol's condition became too unstable for me to leave him at all, a friend who helped me with cleaning invited me to attend her church. She knew that I had been unable to attend my own church for a long while. I so appreciated her gesture, and indeed, I was able to attend her church twice.

A women's study group there was focusing on the subject of establishing and maintaining healthy marriage relationships. The leaders felt sure that I would have some sage advice since Karol and I had been married fifty-four years; so they invited me to speak about our life together. Had Karol been with me, he no doubt could have provided more balance to the presentation. He surely modeled well how to honor his vow to remain faithful in sickness and in health. I emphasized the importance of forgiveness, not only of spouse and family, but to anyone who we've hurt, or those who have hurt us. The pastor at that church and his wife visited our home several times during my husband's last days, and I continue to hold a warm spot in my heart for their hospitality and caring.

Always the fun guy, Karol still liked to tease me. Since he had been forced to give up cigarettes, he rebelled by not shaving. His beard and mustache grew wild and Santa-Claus-like. "Now," he said, "complaints toward my cigarette smoking can be redirected toward my unshaven face." On one of his better days he mischievously kissed me and rubbed that long, wiry beard all over my face. I let him know in no uncertain terms that all future kisses would have to be thrown to me.

Hospice came to visit, and seeing the level of care that I was attempting to give Karol on my own, they strongly suggested that I get help. Their fear was that the stress would cause me to revert to racing thoughts and mood swings. They could not imagine that I was holding up so well under sleep deprivation, and the stress of watching my husband's deteriorating condition and constant struggle for breath. In reality, I was prepared for his passing, and I was as calm and peaceful as could be. I had been shielded from a lot of things growing up, but I learned first hand that death is a part of life. I also knew that God would walk with me through the valley.

Just prior to Thanksgiving in 2008 my physical exhaustion was apparent. Our daughter, Debbie found a strong male caregiver to care for Karol during daytime hours. He also did all of our cooking. This allowed me to sleep during the day knowing that Karol was getting good care. Then I could assume his care throughout the night. I had agreed to the plan, but despite having enjoyed the excellent help, I chose to go back to caring for Karol by myself after the Thanksgiving holiday was behind us.

Karol seemed a bit weaker on Christmas Day. However, our daughter, Karol Ann, who lives in town, and our grandchildren were all with us that day. They came by often to look in on us, but this day was especially poignant in that we all knew it would be Karol's last Christmas. Friends brought our dinner on the following day and there was little left over. Just enough congealed salad was left for Karol to eat the next day. While I was preparing dinner the next evening Karol asked if Karol Ann would be coming tonight. Before finishing with dinner, I made myself a note to call her as soon as I could to tell her that her dad had asked about her.

It is amazing how we recall every small action leading up to a major crisis. I recall putting the left-over gelatin on a table by Karol's bedside and starting back to the kitchen to bring the rest of his food. It was then that I heard his panicked call for oxygen. I rushed back to his side and found that he was connected to the oxygen supply, but he continued to beg for oxygen. I pushed the emergency button which alerted the house staff that immediate medical help was needed. Help arrived seconds later and emergency medics were called. The staff help also remained with me until the paramedics arrived.

Meanwhile we wondered if there was a problem with the oxygen unit. At that point, I ran to get the spare portable unit. As I reached across Karol to connect it, he fell unconscious into my arms. At just that moment, the paramedics arrived. They immediately put him on a stretcher and began administering CPR. Continuing to work on him, they rushed him down the hall and out of the building to transport him to the hospital. He didn't live to get there.

The Lord was with me during that time. I was calm on the way to the hospital, as I made funeral arrangements, and during the visitation and funeral. The old Ann who melted down at the slightest thing was not present throughout this difficult time, nor has she been present at any time in the years since. Following the funeral, I went out of town two weeks to stay with my daughter and her family. Their home is in a rural area of the state where peace and quiet reigns. The solitude was balm to my soul. When I returned home, I moved to a lovely one-bedroom apartment in the same complex as before. It is comfortable and affordable.

Four months after Karol's death I was diagnosed with breast cancer and underwent a mastectomy. No chemotherapy was required and I recovered remarkably fast. It is fair to say that I have been through fire, and it has refined me spiritually.[19] Borrowing the title of a famous hymn, I can truly say, "All Is Well with My Soul." Writing this book has been pure joy. I am living proof that persevering in faith is well worth the effort.

Epilogue

I began writing this book about twelve years ago. It became obvious that the timing was not right then, so I put it aside, knowing that I would resume writing at some point down the road. Meanwhile I lost my husband and mother. Their deaths came close together, but several years after my recovery. I am thankful that they were with me during some of the best years of my life when the mood swings had ceased. Widowed and living alone for the first time in my life, I found that a careful ordering of my days left little time for loneliness and self-pity.

I developed a daily routine that fills each waking hour. I wake up at 5:00 a.m. and immediately make my bed so that I am less tempted to return to it before my evening bedtime. The first agenda item is prayer, meditation, and Bible study. My extensive prayer list now includes you, my readers. This is followed by a healthy breakfast. God recently placed on my heart the need to get serious about my diet.

Not a day too soon, I resurrected an old diet that I had been given when first diagnosed with diabetes. It didn't take long until I was in the habit of counting carbs. The resulting weight loss permitted my diabetes medicine to be reduced by two thirds. I also receive vitamin B12 injections regularly. My renewed energy and weight loss also comes from walking all four residential floors of my building every day. Plus, I participate in an exercise program available within the complex. While walking throughout the building, I stop and visit with as many of the other residents as I can. Most are grateful that someone takes time to talk with them. I seek out those who have serious health issues, and encourage them in any way that I can. Loneliness is all too common in a community of senior citizens.

I attend Sunday school and worship each Sunday morning. In the afternoon, I go to the chapel service in my building. Throughout the week I attend prayer groups and women's studies when they are offered. Some of the residents where I live do not have a personal relationship with Jesus. At every opportunity, I share my own faith with them and leave it up to God to use what I have said to accomplish his ends. Many seem fascinated when I share my long struggle with bipolar disorder. They are amazed that I am always happy and positive. Often someone will say, "I would never have guessed that you are bipolar." I give God all of the glory and honor for what He has done in my life.

Squeezed within all of my daily activities, I clean my apartment, prepare my meals and do my laundry. By 6:30 p.m. I am tired and ready to retire to my apartment for a light dinner, and perhaps a bit of reading or television. If I am not too tired, I make a few phone calls to friends and family. Typically, I am ready for bed at 10:00 p.m. As I lie down, the following verse from Psalm 46 often comes to mind, "Be still and know that I am God."[20] I quickly fall asleep and sleep soundly until morning.

My desire is that each person who reads my story finds comfort and hope in the knowledge that God, most often in collaboration with individuals, comforts, assures and heals us no matter how impossible our situation may seem. Regardless of our physical, mental, relational or emotional situation, our journey toward wholeness requires perseverance. Patient and compassionate individuals who stand by to support us in our quests are immensely beneficial. God's primary reason for creating us is that He wants to be in relationship with us. All who seek Him in their lives can expect a better life than they ever could have dreamed of.[21]

Romans 3:10-13 explains the consequences of being without Christ in our lives; the love that Christ has for all of us despite the condition of our heart; and His invitation for us all to receive his gift of salvation.[22] In addition, we need regular spiritual checkups that require a personal spiritual inventory. This is best accomplished by being in regular communion with other believers who hold each other accountable. Before we go to sleep each night, we need to make an examination of conscience. ". . . *so then just as you received Christ Jesus as Lord, continue to live in him, rooted and built up in him, strengthened in the faith as you were taught, and overflowing with thankfulness.*"[23]

Grace and peace,
Ann Perkins

Suggested Resources

ONLINE SUPPORT, INFORMATION AND SERVICES:

Mental Health Organizations by State: www.cdc.gov/mentalhealth/state_orgs.htm

The National Alliance on Mental Illness

www.nami.org

www.info@nami.org for state and local affiliate organizations

The National Institute of Mental Health:

www.nimh.nih.gov/health/publications/bipolar-disorder

Peer Specialist Services : Search the web for Peer Specialist Services using keywords: "Mental Health Association of (your state)." Peer Specialists have themselves recovered from a mental health condition and are trained to work within accepted standards of clinical practice. Peer specialists offer hope because they are walking, talking examples of recovery. Twenty-six states offer some peer support services. KPS Services have seen remarkable outcomes in Kentucky since 2008 where Louisville has reduced hospitalizations by 45%.

BOOKS FOR BIPOLAR PATIENTS, THEIR FAMILIES AND PARTNERS:

Bipolar disorder: A guide for patients and families, Second Edition, A Johns Hopkins Press Health Book, Frances Mark Mondimore, MD

The Bipolar Relationship: How to understand, help and love your partner, by Jon P. Block, PHD, Bernard Golden, PHD and Nancy Rosenfeld

BOOKS FOR SPIRITUAL GROWTH:

Baggett, John F	*Times of Tragedy and Moments of Grace*
Jones, E. Stanley	*How to Be A Transformed Person*
Jones, E. Stanley	*Abundant Living*
Lewis, C. S.	*Mere Christianity*
Merton, Thomas	*New Seeds of Contemplation*
Peck, M. Scott	*The Road Less Traveled*
Powell, John	*Fully Human, Fully Alive*
Powell, John	*Why Am I Afraid To Tell You Who I Am*
Schuler, Robert	*Love Yourself and Come Alive*
Strobel, Lee	*The Case for Christ*

DEVOTIONAL BOOKS:

Blackaby, Henry	*Experiencing God Day-By-Day: the Devotional and Journal*
Chambers, Oswald	*My Utmost for His Highest*
Cowman, L. B.	*Streams in the Desert*
Russell, Joy	*God Calling*
Stanley, Charles	*Living Close to God*
Upper Room Devotional	*Varied Devotionals by Volunteer Authors*

Notes

1. Proverbs 23:7, The Holy Bible, King James Version
2. Wikipedia.org/wiki/The Dukes of Hazard
3. John 3:16 *NIV Study Bible*, Anniversary Edition, 1995 by Zondervan Publishing House, Grand Rapids, MI 49530, USA
4. Ephesians 4:26 *NIV Study Bible*, Anniversary Edition, 1995 by Zondervan Publishing House, Grand Rapids, MI 49530, USA
5. Essay TO MY HALLIE, Karol Marie, Self-Actualization, April 7, 1997
6. Mental Illness 101, Angeline J. O'Malley, Christian Social Action, p. 29-31, October 1966
7. Psalm 46:1, *NIV Study Bible*, Anniversary Edition, 1995 by Zondervan Publishing House, Grand Rapids, MI 49530, USA
8. Psalm 46:10, *NIV Study Bible*, Anniversary Edition, 1995 by Zondervan Publishing House, Grand Rapids, MI 49530, USA
9. Public Domain, Frederick M. Lehman | Meir Ben Isaac Nehorai
10. Pamphlet, *History of the Song, The Love of God*, by Fredrick M. Lehman, 1948
11. II Corinthians, 12:7, *NIV Study Bible*, Anniversary Edition, 1995 by Zondervan Publishing House, Grand Rapids, MI 49530, USA
12. John 10:10b, *NIV Study Bible*, Anniversary Edition, 1995 by Zondervan Publishing House, Grand Rapids, MI 49530, USA
13. Galatians 5:22, *NIV Study Bible*, Anniversary Edition, 1995 by Zondervan Publishing House, Grand Rapids, MI 49530, USA
14. World Wide Web, Wikipedia, Thomas Merton Biography, Excerpt June 11, 2010

15 1 Chronicles 4:10, New International Version, Zondervan Publishing House, Grand Rapids, MI, 1995
16 Philippians 4:8, New International Version Study Bible, Zondervan Publishing House, Grand Rapids, MI, 1995
17 Synopsis of teaching, *Recognizing and Dealing with the Enemy*, Letter from Craig Marsh, June 11, 2010
18 Colossians 2, New International Version Study Bible, Zondervan Publishing House, Grand Rapids, MI, 1995
19 Isaiah 48:10, New International Version Study Bible, Zondervan Publishing House, Grand Rapids, MI, 1995
20 Psalm 46:10, New International Version Study Bible, Zondervan Publishing House, Grand Rapids, MI, 1995
21 John 20:10, The Message Bible in Contemporary Language, Eugene Peterson Alive Communications, Colorado Springs, CO, 2002
22 Romans 3:10-13, New International Version Study Bible, Zondervan Publishing House, Grand Rapids, MI, 1995
23 Colossians 2:67, New International Version Study Bible, Zondervan Publishing House, Grand Rapids, MI, 1995

CPSIA information can be obtained
at www.ICGtesting.com
Printed in the USA
BVHW040320300523
665069BV00017B/124